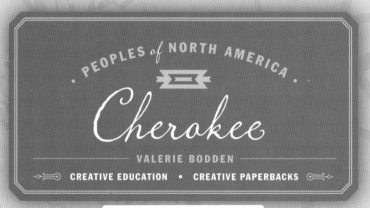

· PEOPLES of NORTH AMERICA ·

Cherokee

VALERIE BODDEN

CREATIVE EDUCATION · CREATIVE PAPERBACKS

Published by Creative Education and Creative Paperbacks
P.O. Box 227, Mankato, Minnesota 56002
Creative Education and Creative Paperbacks
are imprints of The Creative Company
www.thecreativecompany.us

Design and production by Christine Vanderbeek
Art direction by Rita Marshall
Printed in Malaysia

Photographs by Alamy (Everett Collection Historical, Florilegius, Robert W. Ginn, History
Archives, Niday Picture Library, North Wind Picture Archives, Anne Rippy, Running Whirlwind,
Terry Smith Images), Cherokee Phoenix Newspaper, Corbis (Tony Arruza, Bettmann, Burstein
Collection, Christie's Images, Corbis, Paul Damien/National Geographic Society, Kevin Fleming,
Raymond Gehman, Danny Lehman, Joe McDonald, Michael S. Quinton/National Geographic
Society, Peter Turnley), iStockphoto (foofie, Eric Isselée, KirsanovV), Shutterstock (jadimages,
Doug James, MidoSemsem, OHishiapply, Transia Design, Jerry Whaley)

Library of Congress Cataloging-in-Publication Data
Bodden, Valerie.
Cherokee / Valerie Bodden.
p. cm. — (Peoples of North America) • Includes bibliographical references and index.
Summary: A history of the people and events that influenced the North American Indian tribe
known as the Cherokee, including chief John Ross and conflicts surrounding the Trail of Tears.
ISBN 978-1-60818-551-1 (hardcover)
ISBN 978-1-62832-152-4 (pbk)
1. Cherokee Indians—Juvenile literature. I. Title.

E99.C5B57 2015
975.004'97557—dc23   2014041745

CCSS: RI.5.1, 2, 3, 5, 6, 8, 9; RH.6-8.4, 5, 6, 7, 8, 9

First Edition HC 9 8 7 6 5 4 3 2 1
First Edition PBK 9 8 7 6 5 4 3 2 1

PEOPLES *of* NORTH AMERICA

Cherokee

VALERIE BODDEN

CREATIVE EDUCATION • CREATIVE PAPERBACKS

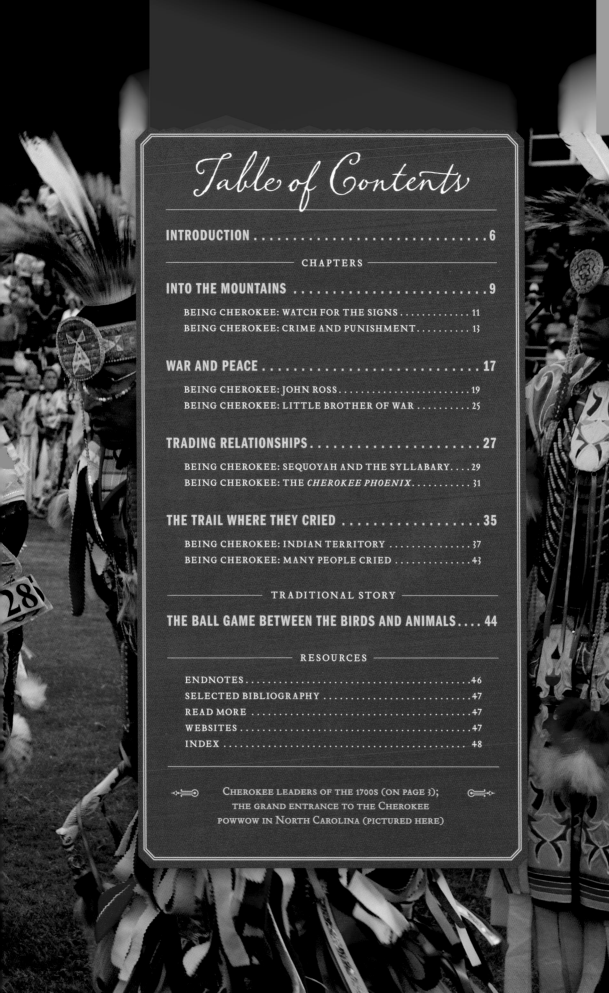

Table of Contents

CHEROKEE LEADERS OF THE 1700S (ON PAGE 3);
THE GRAND ENTRANCE TO THE CHEROKEE
POWWOW IN NORTH CAROLINA (PICTURED HERE)

The Cherokee Indians called their homeland in the mountains of southeastern North America *Shaconage*, meaning "place of blue smoke." The name came from the low, blue haze that seemed draped over the rounded peaks today known as the Blue Ridge and Great Smoky Mountains. Dense forests of oak, hemlock, and poplar blanketed the mountainsides, and the air was thick with the scent of pine. Squirrels, mice, and rabbits scurried through the underbrush, while birds flitted through the trees, calling out their alarm when predators approached. Elk, deer, bears, and turkeys ranged through the forests, providing game for the Cherokee, who also farmed. The rich land gave the Cherokee everything they needed. To them, it was enchanted.

The Cherokee called themselves *Ani-yunwi-ya* or *Tsalagi*, names that mean "Real People" or "Principal People." The word "Cherokee" may have come from an English interpretation of the word *Tsalagi*. Or it may have originated with a Creek name meaning "people of a different speech" or a Choctaw word meaning "cave people." Over time, though, the Real People accepted the name Cherokee. They also accepted many of the ways of the white people who settled on and near their lands beginning in the late 1600s. Even so, the Cherokee were forcibly removed from their lands and made to resettle in the present-day state of Oklahoma. There they established a new nation—one that held on to much of their traditional culture even while adapting to the new ways of the people around them.

THE GREAT SMOKIES ACTED AS A BARRIER BETWEEN CHEROKEE SETTLEMENTS IN TENNESSEE.

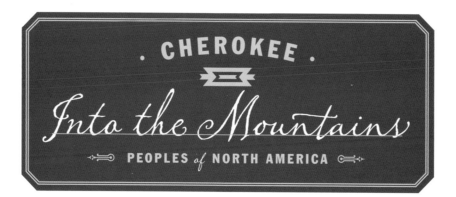

CHEROKEE

Into the Mountains

PEOPLES of NORTH AMERICA

The Cherokee probably arrived in the southeastern corner of North America sometime between A.D. 1000 and 1500. But **ANTHROPOLOGISTS** are divided over where the Cherokee's ancestors lived before that time. Some believe the Cherokee were once part of the Iroquoian Indian groups that lived near the Great Lakes. As evidence, they point to the Cherokee language, which is part of the Iroquoian language family, as well as to traditions the Cherokee held in common with the Iroquois. Other anthropologists believe the Cherokee have more in common with native South American tribes, whose basket-weaving techniques are similar to those of the Cherokee. They say that the Cherokee may have migrated north from lands in South America.

Wherever they came from, the Cherokee spread to claim lands in parts of the present-day states of North and South Carolina, Tennessee, Georgia, Kentucky, Virginia, West Virginia, and Alabama. Within these lands, the Cherokee settled into 60 to 80 widely scattered towns. Although the Cherokee people were connected by a common culture and language, the towns were located in four separate regions, and the people of each region spoke a different **DIALECT** of the Cherokee language. The Cherokee towns of western

A SEVEN-POINTED STAR REPRESENTING THE SEVEN CLANS WAS FEATURED ON CEREMONIAL CLOTHING AND OTHER MATERIALS.

NOT ONLY CARE-
TAKERS OF CHIL-
DREN AND HOMES,
CHEROKEE WOMEN
HELD CENTRAL
POSITIONS IN CLAN
ORGANIZATION.

South Carolina and eastern Georgia were known as the Lower Settlements. Those along the Little Tennessee and Tuckasegee Rivers of North Carolina made up the Middle Settlements. The towns of western North Carolina were part of the Valley Settlements, while those in eastern Tennessee were known as the Overhill Settlements. The different areas were connected by networks of trails, and the various dialects were close enough to be mutually understood.

In all Cherokee towns, the people were divided into the same seven clans: Wolf, Deer, Bird, Red Paint, Blue, Wild Potato, and Twisters (or Long Hair). The members of a clan were part of an extended family—parents and children, as well as grandparents, aunts, uncles, and cousins. Clans were matrilineal, meaning that family relationships were traced through the female line. So children belonged to the same clan as their mother, not their father. Because they were part of the same family, members of a clan could not marry one another. When a couple got married, they lived with the wife's clan. Each clan took care of its own members. Whenever someone visited another town, the members of his or her clan in that town would provide shelter and food.

Most Cherokee towns were built along rivers, which provided a source of fish, fertile land for farming, good hunting grounds, and water for ceremonies. A town was usually surrounded by a fence made of thick, pointed logs to provide protection from enemies. A council house sat at the center of the town on top of a mound made of dirt. The circle-shaped council house was 50 to 60 feet (15.2–18.3 m) across—large enough to hold the entire town's population of 200 to 400 people—and had a cone-shaped roof. Inside, seven sections of benches—one for each clan—surrounded a sacred fire at the center. The fire was never allowed to

Being Cherokee

✦⇒ **WATCH FOR THE SIGNS** ⇐✦ *As they went about their everyday lives, Cherokees were always on the alert for certain signs that signaled things to come— usually death or illness. Signs that a family member would die included seeing a fox that ran a few steps, then looked back and barked; frightening a wolf; seeing two fighting squirrels fall out of a tree and die; or hearing a hen crow. Many of the signs were un- likely or impossible, but they helped the Cherokee accept otherwise unexplainable deaths.*

go out. Along with government meetings, the council house hosted religious ceremonies, feasts, and social events. Near the council house was a large open area called the "square ground" on which dances and other ceremonies were held. The square ground was surrounded by seven roofed shelters to provide shade to each clan. There was also a community storehouse that was stocked with food in preparation for festivals. In some towns, a second open-air council house was used in the summer months.

The families of a clan built their homes near each other. Borders of stones, sticks, or dirt hills separated the different clans. Many families had two homes—one for use in the summer and one for the winter. The summer home was usually rectangular, with a roof of **THATCH** or bark. Some summer houses were left open to the air. Others had walls that were made by weaving flexible branches or river cane through upright support posts. The walls were then coated with a mixture of mud, clay, and grass. Sometimes, they were painted with a whitewash made of crushed clam shells. The summer house might have a few small windows or no windows at all. Inside, small log beds elevated slightly off the floor lined the walls. Cane mats and animal skins provided

CRIME AND PUNISHMENT *Before the 1800s, the Cherokee did not have a written law code. Each clan administered its own justice. If a member of one clan killed a member of another clan, the people of the victim's clan sought blood vengeance by killing someone from the killer's clan. In order to avoid blood vengeance, the members of the murderer's clan might kill him themselves. If the crime had been accidental, the members of the killer's clan might instead give the victim's clan an enemy* **SCALP.**

comfort and warmth. Baskets and clay pots stored food and other supplies, and colorful rugs decorated the dirt floor.

The winter house, also called a hothouse, was generally dome-shaped and much smaller than the summer house. The window-less walls were plastered with six or seven inches (15.2–17.8 cm) of mud and clay to keep out the cold mountain winds. The roof might be covered with thick thatch, bark, or more layers of mud. A fire was lit at the center of the hothouse, which had a small hole in the roof to let out smoke. The fire was allowed to die down at night, when the hole in the roof and a flap over the door were closed. The room got so warm that blankets were rarely needed. Benches along the walls of the hothouse served as beds. In the late 1700s, many Cherokees replaced their traditional summer and winter homes with log cabins.

Each family's dwelling site also included a garden. Larger fields were located both within and outside the town's walls. Each family had its own section in these fields, but Cherokee women worked all the sections together. The Cherokee's most important crop was corn, but they also grew beans, melons, pumpkins, peas, and squash. In addition to farming, the Cherokee gathered wild

CHEROKEE WOMEN
HAVE FARMED
FLINT CORN SINCE
ABOUT A.D. 900
AND CONTINUE
TO TEACH THEIR
WEAVING SKILLS
TODAY.

plants such as nuts, fruits, onions, mushrooms, and grapes. They obtained meat by hunting deer, elk, bison, and turkey.

Other southeastern Indian tribes noticed the abundance of the Cherokee's lands, and they often tried to take over the territory for themselves. The Cherokee, too, tried to expand their holdings by taking over the lands of other tribes. They were often at war with neighboring peoples such as the Creek, Seneca, Shawnee, Chickasaw, and Catawba. Even so, the Cherokee allied with some of these tribes on occasion to take on a common enemy and formed trade relationships with others. They still traded with tribes with whom they were at war by arranging the trade through other tribes, such as the Choctaws or the Chitimachas.

By the 1600s, the Cherokee were among the largest nations of southeastern North America, with a population numbering around 22,000. They controlled some 40,000 square miles (103,600 sq m) of land. The land fed them, and its mountains protected them from outsiders. Traditional Cherokee stories told of how the Cherokee had been the first to settle in these mountains. And they trusted that as long as they continued to respect and take care of the land, it would always be theirs.

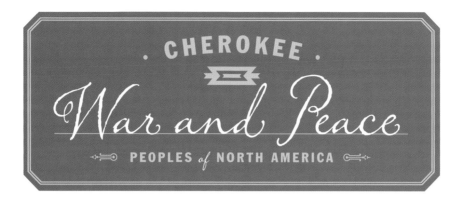

The Cherokee life was divided between times of war and times of peace. Reflecting this fact, each Cherokee town had two chiefs. One was a white, or peace, chief, while the other was a red, or war, chief. The white chief oversaw the everyday life of the town and also served as its high priest. The red chief led the town during times of war and in negotiations with outsiders. Each chief had a number of councilors and officials who served with him. The majority were men, but a group of "Beloved Women" took part in war councils and was responsible for determining the treatment of prisoners taken in war. Neither the white nor the red chief ruled on his own. Rather, they sought a **CONSENSUS** among their councilors.

Each town made its own decisions and acted independently of the rest. But the towns also came together to form a national government. Like the towns, the Cherokee national government had a white and a red chief with his own officials and councilors. The position of white chief was hereditary, but it did not pass from father to son. Instead, the oldest son of the chief's oldest sister became the next white chief. The red chief was usually a man who had proven himself in battle, and he was chosen by popular vote. The national chiefs often consulted with the town chiefs on the most important decisions.

THE 18TH-CENTURY CHEROKEE WAR CHIEF OSTENACO WAS AN EARLY BRITISH ALLY, EVEN VISITING LONDON IN 1762.

A WARRIOR KNOWN
AS DUTCH (ABOVE)
FAMOUSLY BATTLED
THE OSAGE BUT
ALSO LIVED AMONG
THAT ENEMY TRIBE
FOR A TIME.

As in the towns, the national government ruled by consensus. But its decisions were not necessarily binding. If a town's chiefs decided they didn't agree with the decisions of the national government, they might decide not to follow them.

National council meetings, which lasted several days and included dances, games, and feasts, were held in the national capital. At first, the capital was not a fixed location; whenever a new white chief was selected, his town became the capital. But in 1827, the town of New Echota in present-day Georgia became the permanent Cherokee capital. Leaders and visitors from towns across the Cherokee Nation traveled to the capital for council meetings. The meetings were held in the national heptagon, a 7-sided council building that could seat more than 1,000 people. As in the towns, the people were seated by clan. The national heptagon was also used for celebrating national festivals and assembling national war parties.

Wars were generally fought in the spring, summer, and fall, when the weather was warmer. They often involved conflicts with neighboring tribes, but at times, the Cherokee marched east to the Atlantic coast or north to the Ohio River to fight. Wars were fought for a number of reasons. If another tribe had attacked or killed Cherokees, a war party was assembled to take revenge on that tribe. If enemies posed a threat near a town, that town or the entire nation might be called to war. Sometimes, an enemy would challenge the Cherokees to war, and they would meet at a designated time and place to fight.

No matter the motive, nearly all wars began by observing

Being Cherokee

⟶ JOHN ROSS ⟵ Born in 1790 to a Scottish father and mixed-blood mother, John Ross was only one-eighth Cherokee. Ross was educated at a boarding school and later became a wealthy trader and **PLANTATION** owner. Although he spoke little Cherokee and wore a suit and tie, his dedication to the Cherokee Nation impressed even full-blood Cherokees. He was elected the Cherokee Nation's first principal chief in 1828. He continued to serve in that role until his death in 1866, making him the longest-serving principal chief in Cherokee history.

several days of rituals, including prayers, **FASTS**, and a special purifying drink. When they reached the enemy's country, Cherokee warriors shouted war whoops as they ran into battle. Cherokee weapons included bows and arrows, war clubs, axes, knives, and lances. Warriors defended themselves with hardened bison-skin shields. In some cases, they took the scalps of their enemies following the battle.

During the late fall and winter, the men turned from making war to hunting. As when marching to war, men had to undergo a number of rituals before participating in a hunt. All men hunted to provide food for their families, but a few became hunting specialists. These men were professional hunters who provided game for festivals and religious ceremonies. They had to complete an intense training period, and when they hunted, they followed even more elaborate rituals than other hunters so that the meat they obtained would be acceptable.

Hunters used a bow and arrow to bring down bison, deer, squirrels, turkeys, and pheasants. They also carried a blowgun for smaller game, such as rabbits and small birds. The blowgun was 3 to 12 feet (0.9–3.7 m) long and shot darts made of sharp wood. A hunter might have to walk 30 miles (48.3 km) or more through the mountains over the course of a hunt.

While a man went to war and took part in hunting expeditions, his wife took care of the house, which she owned. She spent most of her time cooking and tending the fields. Women also made the family's clothing from deer and bear skins and wove baskets from river cane tinted with vegetable dyes. In addition, women were responsible for caring for young children. Cherokee children learned by watching and imitating. They were generally indulged and were never physically disciplined.

In everything they did, the Cherokee were aware of the

UNTIL THEY CAME IN CONTACT WITH EUROPEAN GUNS, THE TRIBES OF NORTH AMERICA MADE USE OF THE BOW AND ARROW.

spiritual world. They talked of a Great Spirit, or Creator, and believed that there was spiritual power in everything, including the sun, fire, water, animals, plants, rivers, and mountains. Priests oversaw Cherokee spiritual life, and they were trusted to provide the answer for illness, poor crops, and other troubles. Young boys whose family members had been priests might be promised to the priesthood at birth. Twins or boys born when there were certain signs in the stars might be promised as priests, too. These boys began their training around the age of 9 or 10, when an experienced priest taught them the prayers that would bring blessings to the people. The priest also taught the boy the secrets of his divining crystals, which the Cherokee believed could predict the outcome of a hunt, find lost objects, or determine whether a person would fall ill.

Every year, the Cherokee observed six major ceremonies in the national capital. People from all the towns journeyed through the mountains to take part, swelling the capital's population to 10,000

LITTLE BROTHER OF WAR *When they weren't hunting or at war, Cherokee men liked to play stickball, a game so rough that it was called the "little brother of war." Each stickball team had 10 to 14 players who each carried 3-foot-long (0.9 m) sticks with webbing on the end. Players used the sticks to pick up, catch, and throw a ball. Teams tried to score goals by driving the ball between two posts at the end of a field. The first team to score 12 goals won.*

or more. Every festival involved dancing to music made by gourd and turtleshell rattles and water drums. For some festivals, only the men danced; for others, the women joined in. During some of the festivals, all participants were required to immerse themselves in the river, fully clothed, seven times. Or the participants might have to fast or stay awake all night. Among the most important festivals each year was the Green Corn Festival, held in celebration of the corn harvest.

In addition to the major festivals, other dances were held to prepare for or celebrate various events. Eagle dances were held to seek strength for war, and the Scalp Dance celebrated a war victory. The Peace Pipe Dance was held when the Cherokee declared peace with an enemy. The Booger Dance was a lighthearted event in which the dancers wore gourd masks and made fun of the Cherokee's enemies. Other festivals honored the new moon or a successful hunt.

DANCERS KEEP NATIVE TRADITIONS ALIVE AT FESTIVALS AROUND THE COUNTRY, FROM GEORGIA (PAGE 23) TO ARIZONA (OPPOSITE).

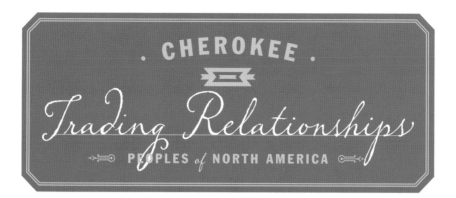

CHEROKEE
Trading Relationships
PEOPLES of NORTH AMERICA

The first European explorers arrived in North America in the early 1500s, and it wasn't long before they encountered the Cherokee. Around 1540, a Spanish expedition led by Hernando de Soto visited several Cherokee towns. The Cherokee greeted the newcomers and gave them food but had little further contact with Europeans for the next century.

Then, in the late 1600s, British traders began to travel into Cherokee country, seeking deerskins and other furs to send back to Europe. They traded these for European goods such as kettles, hatchets, hoes, knives, guns, and whiskey. Many of the traders settled in the Cherokee towns, and a number even married Cherokee women. Their half-Cherokee and half-European children were later referred to as mixed-bloods, but they were still considered part of the Cherokee Nation.

Interaction with European traders changed the life of the Cherokee in another way—it brought new diseases. Since the Indians had never been exposed to diseases such as smallpox before, their bodies had no defense against them. From the late 1600s through the mid-1700s, smallpox epidemics swept through Cherokee towns. The outbreaks, combined with warfare, reduced the population from an estimated 35,000 in 1697 to about 12,000 by 1770.

LIKE THE CHEROKEE, OTHER TRIBES OF THE
EASTERN WOODLANDS MET EUROPEAN NEWCOM-
ERS WITH SIGNS OF PEACE.

SMALLPOX HAD A DEVASTATING EFFECT ON NOT ONLY THE CHEROKEE BUT OTHER TRIBES (SUCH AS THE WAMPANOAG) AS WELL.

Throughout the 1700s, more and more European settlers built homes on or near Cherokee lands. In 1721, the Cherokee signed their first treaty with the settlers. The treaty established the borders of Cherokee country, but it also gave some Cherokee land to the British. Over the next 50 years, the Cherokee made several additional agreements with the British. In each one, they gave up land. The lands traded away were generally Cherokee hunting grounds that white settlers had already taken over.

In 1754, the French and Indian War began. Britain and its Indian partners were pitted against France, which had its own Indian allies. The Cherokee agreed to fight on the side of the British, with whom they had trade agreements. Historians estimate that between 100 and 1,000 Cherokee warriors fought for the British. But to many British soldiers, all Indians were the same, and they burned the fields of any native town they passed through, even those of the Cherokee. In return, angry Cherokee warriors left their alliance with the British and returned home. Some Cherokees stole horses and other goods from nearby settlers. The settlers retaliated by killing and scalping the warriors. These acts led to the outbreak of the Anglo-Cherokee War in 1759. For three years, each side attacked the other's settlements and towns, killing many.

The French and Indian and Anglo-Cherokee wars ended in the 1760s. But the Cherokee continued to have problems with white settlers on Cherokee lands. Cherokee chief Dragging Canoe worried about what this meant for the future of his people. "The white men have almost surrounded us, leaving us only a little spot of ground to stand upon, and it seems to be their intention to destroy us as a nation," he said.

SEQUOYAH AND THE SYLLABARY *A mixed-blood Cherokee, Sequoyah (also called George Guess) was born around 1760 or 1765. Although Sequoyah did not attend school, he was intrigued by the white people's ability to communicate through writing. He figured out that the Cherokee language could be broken down into 86 syllables, and he created written symbols to represent each syllable. In 12 years, Sequoyah completed the Cherokee* **SYLLABARY,** *and then he traveled through Cherokee lands to teach it to others. Sequoyah remains the only person to single-handedly invent a written language.*

ᏣᎳᎩ ᏚᎴᎯᏌᏃᎢ

CHEROKEE PHOENIX.

VOL. I.   NEW ECHOTA, WEDNESDAY MAY 21, 1828.   **NO.**

EDITED BY ELIAS BOUDINOTT,
PRINTED WEEKLY BY
ISAAC H. HARRIS,
FOR THE CHEROKEE NATION.

At $2.50 if paid in advance, $3 in six months, or $3.50 if paid at the end of the year.

To subscribers who can read only the Cherokee language the price will be $2,00 in advance, or $2,50 to be paid within the year.

Every subscription will be considered as continued unless subscribers give notice to the contrary before the commencement of a new year.

Any person procuring six subscribers, and becoming responsible for the payment, shall receive a seventh gratis.

Advertisements will be inserted at seventy-five cents per square for the first insertion, and thirty-seven and a half cents for each continuance; longer ones in proportion.

All letters addressed to the Editor, post paid, will receive due attention.

New Town, Nov. 10, 1825.

Resolved by the National Committee and Council, That the children of Cherokee men and white women. living in the Cherokee nation as man and wife, be, and they are hereby acknowledged to be equally entitled to all the immunities and privileges enjoyed by the citizens descending from the Cherokee race, by the mothers side.

By order of the National Committee,
JNO. ROSS, Pres't N. Committee.
MAJOR RIDGE, Speaker.
PATH ⋈ KILLER,
CHARLES HICKS.
A. McCOY, Clerk of the N. Com.
E. BOUDINOTT, Clk. N. Coun.

New Town, Nov. 10, 1824.

Resolved by the National Committee and Council, That the section embraced in the law regulating marriages between white men and Cherokee

which may be left by any person or persons removing to another place, and the improvements so left, remain unoccupied for the term of three years, such improvements shall be considered abandoned, and any other person or persons whatsoever, may take and go in possession of such improvements, in the same manner as if there were no improvements.

By order of the N. Committee,
JNO. ROSS, Pres't. Nat. Com.
PATH ⋈ KILLER,
A. McCOY, Clerk N. Com.
E. BOUDINOTT, Clerk of N. Council.

New Town, Nov. 12, 1825.

Resolved by the National Committee and Council, That all lawful contracts shall be binding, and whenever judgments shall have been obtained from any of the courts of justice in the Cherokee nation, against any person or persons whatsoever, on a plea

---

THE BILINGUAL *CHEROKEE PHOENIX* REACHED PEOPLE BOTH WITHIN AND OUTSIDE THE INDIAN COMMUNITY.

When war broke out between the American colonists and the British crown in 1775, Dragging Canoe decided that the British would do more to defend Cherokee borders than would the colonists. So the Cherokee sided with the British in the American Revolution. Cherokee warriors attacked colonial settlements and forts, and the American **MILITIA** burned Cherokee fields and towns. At war's end, the now independent colonists forced the Cherokee to give up even more land. Treaties signed in the late 1700s and early 1800s reduced Cherokee territory further, until it fell almost entirely within the borders of Georgia.

In 1817, the United States tried to convince the Cherokee to give up their remaining lands and move across the Mississippi River into present-day Arkansas. The federal government promised each man who agreed to resettle a rifle and ammunition, as well as a blanket and a brass kettle or a beaver trap. More than 1,000 agreed to go. Eleven years later, those who had moved to Arkansas were again resettled in Indian Territory (present-day Oklahoma).

But still, government officials weren't satisfied. They wanted the remaining Cherokee to move west, too. A Cherokee delegation firmly denied the request, reminding the American government

⇒ THE *CHEROKEE PHOENIX* ⇐ *The invention of the Cherokee syllabary in 1821 allowed the Cherokee people to start the first American Indian newspaper in the country. The first issue of the* Cherokee Phoenix *was published on February 21, 1828. Written in both Cherokee and English, the newspaper printed local and international news as well as official Cherokee Nation opinion on important issues, such as the Indian Removal Act. A publicity tour by the paper's first editor, Elias Boudinot, garnered subscribers from across the U.S. and Europe.*

that "the Cherokee are not foreigners but original inhabitants of America, and that they now inhabit and stand on the soil of their own territory."

Although they remained in their own territory, life for the Cherokee was changing. While many full-bloods continued to observe traditional practices, by the early 1800s, many mixed-bloods had adopted the lifestyles of the whites who surrounded them. They became full-time farmers, and some even set up large plantations worked by African American slaves. Many Cherokees moved into log houses or, if they were wealthy, Southern plantation-style homes. They dressed like their American neighbors. White missionaries introduced the Christian religion and were invited to build schools on Cherokee lands, or children were sent away to boarding schools.

Soon, many Cherokees could read and write English, and in 1821, a Cherokee named Sequoyah introduced a syllabary of the Cherokee language. The syllabary allowed the language to be written for the first time, and within months of its introduction, many Cherokees could both read and write Cherokee. A Cherokee-language newspaper began publication in February 1828. By the

1830s, Cherokees had become successful merchants, traders, writers, and teachers. Because they had embraced the culture introduced by the whites, Americans referred to them as one of the five "civilized" tribes (along with the Creek, Choctaw, Chickasaw, and Seminole).

Among the biggest changes to the Cherokee lifestyle was its system of government, which was reformed in 1827 to closely mirror that of the U.S. Like the American government, the new Cherokee government had three branches: executive, **LEGISLATIVE**, and judicial. A constitution was written, the capital was established at New Echota, and a mixed-blood Cherokee named John Ross was elected the new Cherokee Nation's first "principal chief" (equivalent to an American president).

The first challenge the new Cherokee government faced was dealing with lawmakers in Georgia who had declared the Cherokee constitution illegal. They said the Cherokee were bound by the laws of Georgia, since their territory fell within the boundaries of the state. Georgian legislators also claimed that the land on which the Cherokee Nation was situated rightfully belonged to the state of Georgia. When gold was discovered on Cherokee lands in 1829, Georgia **ANNEXED** much of that land and began offering sections of it by lottery to its citizens.

U.S. president **ANDREW JACKSON** supported Georgia's claim to the land, believing the Cherokee had "neither the intelligence, the industry, the moral habits, nor the desire of improvement" to make them fit for life among whites. In 1830, Jackson convinced Congress to sign the Indian Removal Act, which gave the president authority to force eastern tribes to relocate to Indian Territory. Within two years, the other four civilized tribes had signed treaties to that effect. But principal chief John Ross resolved that the Cherokee would "remain peaceably and quietly on their own soil."

CHEROKEE

The Trail Where They Cried

PEOPLES *of* NORTH AMERICA

Most Cherokees supported Ross's determination to remain in their homeland. But some, sensing that continuing to fight the U.S. government was futile, began to advocate for removal. One such supporter was Major Ridge, who told the people, "We can never forget these homes, I know, but an unbending, iron necessity tells us we must leave them. I would willingly die to preserve them, but any forcible effort to keep them will cost us our lands, our lives, and the lives of our children." Those Cherokees who favored signing a removal treaty with the U.S. became members of the Treaty Party, led by Major Ridge's son, John Ridge.

In December 1835, members of the Treaty Party met with U.S. officials and signed the Treaty of New Echota, agreeing to sell all Cherokee lands in the East for $5 million and move to Indian Territory. John Ross and others protested that the treaty was illegal, since its signers were not officials of the Cherokee government. Despite the protests, the U.S. Congress voted for the treaty. The deadline for removal was set for May 23, 1838.

By that date, about 2,000 Cherokees had traveled west to Indian Territory. But the rest—about 16,000—remained in their homeland. General Winfield Scott and 7,000 U.S. soldiers were sent to round up the remaining Cherokees.

BORN IN GEORGIA, JOHN RIDGE (OPPOSITE) WAS
EDUCATED IN CONNECTICUT AT THE SAME SCHOOL
AS HIS COUSIN, ELIAS BOUDINOT.

SEVERAL TYPES OF ROADWAY SIGNS MARK THE TRAIL OF TEARS, INCLUDING THOSE BEARING THE WORDS "ORIGINAL ROUTE."

The soldiers marched through the Cherokee Nation in May 1838, pulling people from their fields, dinner tables, and beds and depositing them in hastily built holding forts, where many died of heat, malnutrition, and illness.

In June, a group of about 5,000 Cherokees began the journey west by boat. Many of them died from heat and illness, and the remaining Cherokees requested that the rest of the removals be put off until the weather was cooler. Their request was granted.

At the end of August, the remaining Cherokees began their move west in groups of about 1,000. Groups continued to move out through December. Each group took a roughly similar overland route of more than 800 miles (1,287 km). Most Cherokees traveled on foot, many with no shoes. Winter weather stranded several groups along the Mississippi River. They remained along the riverbank for up to a month, many of them with only a single blanket to offer warmth. Finally, after three to six months on the weary trail, the groups began to arrive in Indian Territory between January and March 1839. An estimated 4,000 Cherokees had died in the holding forts and on the journey west, leading the Cherokee to call their journey "The Trail Where They Cried." Today, it is more commonly known as the "Trail of Tears."

Even as the majority of the Cherokee Nation struggled along the Trail of Tears, a small group that lived outside the Nation in the mountains of North Carolina was granted permission to remain. They were joined by nearly 1,000 refugees who managed to escape the roundup in Georgia. Together, these groups became the Eastern Band of the Cherokee Nation. Most were poor and lived in small log cabins. Although some held to traditional values, many

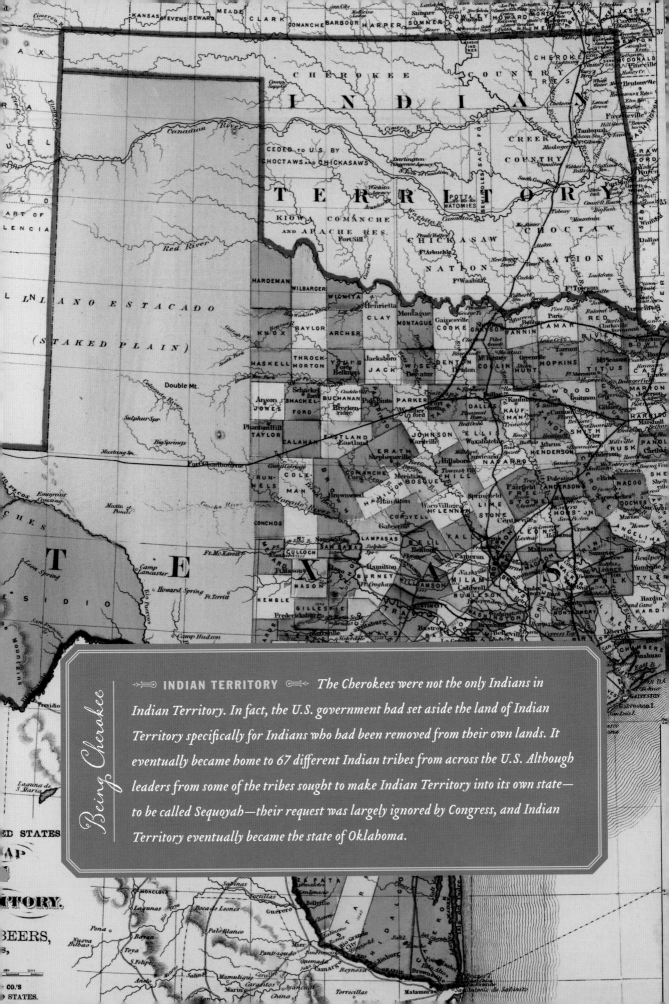

INDIAN TERRITORY ⟐ *The Cherokees were not the only Indians in Indian Territory. In fact, the U.S. government had set aside the land of Indian Territory specifically for Indians who had been removed from their own lands. It eventually became home to 67 different Indian tribes from across the U.S. Although leaders from some of the tribes sought to make Indian Territory into its own state— to be called Sequoyah—their request was largely ignored by Congress, and Indian Territory eventually became the state of Oklahoma.*

Being Cherokee

adopted the white culture that surrounded them.

Meanwhile, in Indian Territory, disagreements arose between the recent arrivals (who were known as the Ross Party) and the Cherokees who had moved there earlier. In the summer of 1839, Major Ridge, John Ridge, and Elias Boudinot were killed for their role in signing the Treaty of New Echota. The murders set off a series of battles between the Treaty Party and the Ross Party. Despite the violence, that year the Cherokee Nation adopted a new constitution and again elected Ross to serve as principal chief. The new Cherokee capital was located in the city of Tahlequah.

In 1846, the Treaty Party and the Ross Party officially declared peace, which marked the beginning of a "Golden Age" for the Cherokee Nation. Many Cherokees became successful merchants and farmers once again. A new Cherokee newspaper began publication. Missionaries established schools on Cherokee lands, and the Cherokee set up their own public school system, including male and female seminaries, or high schools. The Cherokee public school system was widely admired, and whites from the surrounding area even paid to send their children to school there.

The Cherokee Golden Age continued until the beginning of the American Civil War in 1861, which again split the Cherokee Nation. Many Cherokees—especially those who owned slaves—fought on the side of the **CONFEDERACY**. But a number of full-bloods, who called themselves the Keetoowah Society, supported the **UNION**. After the war, the U.S. government forced the Cherokee Nation to give up some of its land in Indian Territory so that newly displaced Indian groups could settle there.

Then, in the early 1900s, the U.S. government dissolved the Cherokee government, made all Cherokees U.S. citizens, and ordered them to enroll for an individual land **ALLOTMENT**. These steps were taken so that the state of Oklahoma could be formed

BEFORE OKLAHOMA BECAME A STATE, THE MIXED POPULATION OF INDIAN TERRITORY BROUGHT VARIOUS PEOPLE TOGETHER.

on Indian Territory in 1907. Many Cherokees adjusted well to the change, becoming prominent politicians in Oklahoma or finding success as artists, writers, actors, teachers, engineers, or architects. Despite such successes, the **GREAT DEPRESSION** and a prolonged drought in the 1930s forced about half of all Cherokees in Oklahoma to leave in search of jobs. Many settled in California, Washington, and Oregon. About 20,000 Cherokees remained in Oklahoma. In the 1970s, the Cherokee Nation's government was restored, and it held its first election for principal chief in more than 60 years.

Today, more than 700,000 people in the U.S. claim Cherokee descent. Most are mixed-bloods. The federal government recognizes three Cherokee tribes: the Cherokee Nation and the United Keetoowah Band in Oklahoma and the Eastern Band of Cherokees in North Carolina. Although many Cherokees have adopted the American lifestyle, they are also dedicated to preserving aspects of their traditional culture. The Cherokee language continues to be spoken by 10,000 to 14,000 people, and classes in the language are offered at schools and universities in communities with large Cherokee populations.

Some modern Cherokee people have also incorporated

Cherokee Alphabet

	R *e*	**T** *i*	**ꮜ** *o*	**O** *u*
Ꭰ *ka*	**Ꮉ** *ge*	**y** *gi*	**A** *go*	**J** *gu*
	Ꭾ *he*	**Ꭿ** *hi*	**Ꮎ** *ho*	**Ꮝ** *hu*
	Ꮷ *le*	**Ꮅ** *li*	**Ꮈ** *lo*	**M** *lu*
	Ꮜ *me*	**H** *mi*	**Ꮕ** *mo*	**y** *mu*
hna **G** *nah*	**Ꮑ** *ne*	**ꮒ** *ni*	**Z** *no*	**ꮘ** *nu*
	ꭥ *que*	**ꮗ** *qui*	**ꮹ** *quo*	**ꮘ** *quu*
s	**4** *se*	**Ᏸ** *si*	**♣** *so*	**Ᏸ** *su*
W *ta*	**Ꮥ** *de* **Ꮤ** *te*	**Ꮑ** *di* **Ꮧ** *ti*	**Ꮣ** *do*	**S** *du*
tla	**L** *tle*	**C** *tli*	**Ꮹ** *tlo*	**Ꮫ** *tlu*
	Ꮳ *tse*	**Ꮳ** *tsi*	**K** *tso*	**Ꮬ** *tsu*
	Ꮺ *we*	**Ᏻ** *wi*	**Ꮼ** *wo*	**Ꮽ** *wu*
	Ᏸ *ye*	**Ꭹ** *yi*	**Ꮵ** *yo*	**G** *yu*

Sounds represented by vowels.

a as *a* in *father* or short as *a* in *rival*
e as *a* in *hate* or short as *e* in *met*
i as *i* in *pique* or short as *i* in *pit*
o as *aw* in *law* or short as *o* in *not*
u as *oo* in *fool* or short as *u* in *pull*
v as *u* in *but*, nasalized.

Consonant Sounds.

in English, but approaching to k._ d nearly as in English, but approaching to t._ h. k. l. m. n. q. s. t. w. y. as
inning with g except & have sometimes the power of k.

MANY PEOPLE CRIED ⟶ *One Cherokee who made the journey on the Trail of Tears later recorded what it was like in these terms: "Long time we travel on way to new land. People feel bad when they leave Old Nation. Women cry and make sad wails. Children cry, and many men cry, and all look sad like when friends died, but they say nothing and just put heads down and keep on going towards West. Many days pass, and people die very much."*

traditional Cherokee clothing into their dress. They practice crafts such as basket-weaving and pottery, and some still attend ritual dances. In both Oklahoma and North Carolina, attractions such as museums, art galleries, outdoor dramas, and recreated Cherokee villages teach tourists about Cherokee life and culture.

As they remember these scenes from the past, the Cherokee people look to the future. "The dreams of our people are woven from a tragic past and difficult present," said former Cherokee Nation principal chief Wilma Mankiller. "Yet those dreams have the ability to continue to guide our people to hope and work for a positive future." The Cherokee way of life has changed much over the past 1,000 years. From their early days hunting and farming in the Blue Ridge and Great Smoky Mountains to their relocation, the Cherokee have adapted at every turn. Today, they embrace their traditions while continuing to adjust to a changing world.

IN CHEROKEE TRADITION AMONG THOSE WHO LIVED IN NORTH CAROLINA, A FATHER PASSED HIS HORSE ON TO HIS SON.

The Cherokee told many stories about the world around them.
Many, like this one, relate how animals came to have certain
features. This story also teaches a lesson about not judging
others based on their size or appearance. In it, the birds
and four-legged animals play each other in one of the
Cherokee's favorite pastimes—the rough game of stickball.

L ong ago, the four-legged animals came together to play a stickball game against the
birds. Mountain Lion, Wolf, Fox, Bobcat, Deer,
and Bear played on the four-legged animals' team. The
birds' team was made up of Hawk, Falcon, Raven, Crow,
Kingfisher, Hummingbird, and Eagle. Before the game
started, two little creatures asked Bear if they could join
the four-legged animals' team. Bear laughed and told
them they were too small. The creatures promised they
would try hard even though they were small, but Bear
sent them away with a growl.

So the creatures went to the birds' team and
asked Eagle if they could join. Eagle replied that
anyone who could fly could join the team. The
creatures were sad because they couldn't fly.
They didn't have wings. But Eagle told
Kingfisher to use his sharp beak to cut
some wings out of leather. Kingfisher

cut them out and attached them to the first creature. Wearing his new wings, the creature climbed to the top of a tree, jumped, and began to fly. He was given the name Bat.

After Bat got his wings, there was not enough leather left to make wings for the second creature. So Eagle had Hawk and Raven each grab the creature's sides and pull. They pulled his skin until it stretched into two flaps. Then Hawk set the creature in a tree and told him to jump. The creature glided through the air. His new name was Flying Squirrel.

The next day, the animals and the birds played stickball from morning to evening. They were evenly matched. First the animals would score, then the birds. Bat and Flying Squirrel watched, but neither touched the ball.

As the sun began to set, the game was tied. It would end with the next score. Deer got the ball for the animals and rushed for the goal. The birds were too tired to stop him. But Flying Squirrel jumped from a tree and glided down to steal the ball from Deer. He passed it to Bat, who flew across the field, dodging the rest of the animals along the way. When he got to the end of the field, he scored the winning goal!

From then on, Bat and Flying Squirrel were so thankful that they could fly that they spent their nights gliding through the trees, waiting for their next chance to play stickball.

ALLOTMENT
a portion set aside for an individual; many American Indians were forced to take allotments from tribal lands, with any remaining lands going to the U.S. government

ANDREW JACKSON
(1767–1845) army general who fought many successful battles against Indian tribes and in 1829 became the country's seventh president; he signed the Indian Removal Act, which relocated Indians to lands west of the Mississippi River

ANNEXED
added land to an existing state or territory

ANTHROPOLOGISTS
people who study the physical traits, cultures, and relationships of different peoples

CONFEDERACY
a group of 11 Southern states that broke away from the United States during the Civil War

CONSENSUS
agreement by all or most of a group

DIALECT
a form of a language that uses specific pronunciations, grammar, or vocabularies that differ from other forms of the language; speakers of different dialects of the same language can usually understand each other

FASTS
periods during which people go without eating, often as part of a religious ritual

GREAT DEPRESSION
a time from 1929 to 1939 when there was widespread unemployment in the U.S. and around the world and a major decline in the production and sale of goods

LEGISLATIVE
related to the lawmaking branch of a government

MILITIA
an army made up of citizens instead of professional soldiers

PLANTATION
a large farm; in the southeastern U.S., plantations grew cotton, tobacco, and rice

SCALP
a portion of the skin at the top of the head, with the attached hair, that was sometimes cut off of an enemy as a battle trophy or to claim a reward

SYLLABARY
a set of written symbols that represent syllables, or parts of a word (rather than individual letters as in an alphabet)

THATCH
straw, reeds, or other plant materials used to cover a roof

UNION
the northern states in the Civil War

Conley, Robert J. *The Cherokee Nation: A History*. Albuquerque: University of New Mexico Press, 2005.

Ehle, John. *Trail of Tears: The Rise and Fall of the Cherokee Nation*. New York: Doubleday, 1988.

Hoxie, Frederick E., ed. *Encyclopedia of North American Indians*. Boston: Houghton Mifflin, 1996.

Josephy, Alvin M. Jr. *500 Nations: An Illustrated History of North American Indians*. New York: Knopf, 1994.

Mails, Thomas E. *The Cherokee People: The Story of the Cherokees from Earliest Origins to Contemporary Times*. Tulsa, Okla.: Council Oak Books, 1992.

Perdue, Theda, and Michael D. Green. *The Cherokee Nation and the Trail of Tears*. New York: Penguin, 2007.

Viola, Herman J. *After Columbus: The Smithsonian Chronicle of the North American Indians*. New York: Orion Books, 1990.

Warhus, Mark. *Another America: Native American Maps and the History of Our Land*. New York: St. Martin's, 1997.

READ MORE

Bjornlund, Lydia. *The Trail of Tears: The Relocation of the Cherokee Nation*. Detroit: Lucent, 2010.

Peppas, Lynn. *Trail of Tears*. New York: Crabtree, 2014.

WEBSITES

CHEROKEE NATION
http://www.cherokee.org/AboutTheNation.aspx
Learn more about Cherokee life today and in the past on the official website of the Cherokee Nation. Check out the language link to learn Cherokee words.

TRAIL OF TEARS NATIONAL HISTORIC TRAIL
http://www.nps.gov/trte/index.htm
The Trail of Tears National Historic Trail passes through nine states along the route many Cherokee took west. The official website includes information and videos about the Cherokees' experiences on the trail.

NOTE: EVERY EFFORT HAS BEEN MADE TO ENSURE THAT THE WEBSITES LISTED ABOVE ARE SUITABLE FOR CHILDREN, THAT THEY HAVE EDUCATIONAL VALUE, AND THAT THEY CONTAIN NO INAPPROPRIATE MATERIAL. HOWEVER, BECAUSE OF THE NATURE OF THE INTERNET, IT IS IMPOSSIBLE TO GUARANTEE THAT THESE SITES WILL REMAIN ACTIVE INDEFINITELY OR THAT THEIR CONTENTS WILL NOT BE ALTERED.